A CATHOLIC BABY RECORD BOOK

by Mary W. Stromwall
Illustrated by Beatrice Ryan

TAN BOOKS AND PUBLISHERS, INC.
Rockford, Illinois 61105

Nihil Obstat: John M. A. Fearns, S.T.D.
                 Censor Librorum

Imprimatur: ✠ Francis Cardinal Spellman
                 Archbishop of New York
                 January 21, 1952

The Nihil Obstat and Imprimatur are official declarations that a book or pamphlet is free of doctrinal or moral error. No implication is contained therein that those who have granted the Nihil Obstat and Imprimatur agree with the contents, opinions or statements expressed.

Copyright © 1952 by Artists and Writers Guild, Inc. Republished with minor revisions by TAN Books and Publishers, Inc. in 2006. Revisions copyright © 2006 by TAN Books and Publishers, Inc.

ISBN   pink cover 0-89555-746-0
       blue cover 0-89555-747-9

Printed and bound in the United States of America.

TAN BOOKS AND PUBLISHERS, INC.
P.O. Box 424
Rockford, Illinois 61105
2006

Foreword

CORNERSTONES are sealed to preserve the record of important buildings erected by men. But a child, the supreme work of God, destined for Eternity with Him, deserves an open record as a remembrance of physical and spiritual development.

Four children of her own and years of experience in motivating children to exert themselves in the service of God qualify Mary W. Stromwall to provide the information in this book.

Parents will welcome *Unto Us a Child Is Given*. It will serve them well as an earthly record of the far more wonderful story in God's Book of Life.

Father Louis A. Gales
Director, Catechetical Guild

𝒢OD has given me a beautiful Guardian Angel,
who watches over me day and night
and keeps my soul and body
safe from harm.

Unto Us A Child Is Given

who shall be called

_____

because _____

_____

Attach first photo here.

I, _____,

was born at _____ a.m. / p.m. on _____

at _____ in _____.

I weighed _____. I was _____ long.

_____ helped bring me into the world.

My Mother's name _____

My Father's name _____

My Birth Certificate

An unsealed envelope containing the Birth Certificate may be attached here. It will be needed in future years for proof of birthplace or age or for other purposes.

Queen of Heaven, Our Blessed Mother

My Baptism

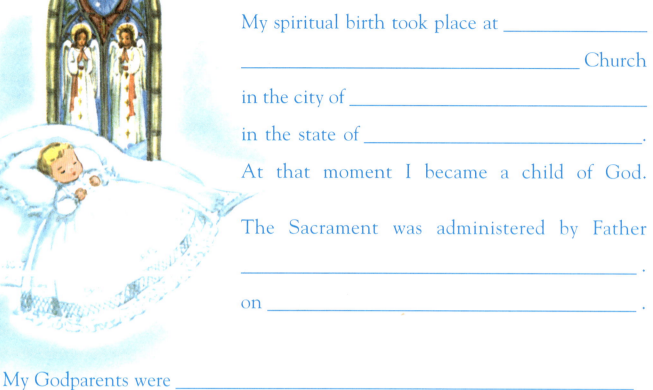

My spiritual birth took place at _____ Church

in the city of _____

in the state of _____.

At that moment I became a child of God.

The Sacrament was administered by Father _____.

on _____.

My Godparents were _____

and _____.

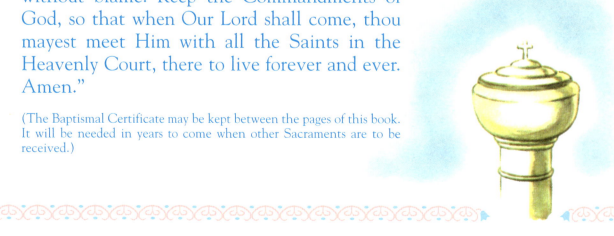

They held a lighted candle for me while Father said, "Receive this burning light and see thou guard the grace of thy Baptism without blame. Keep the Commandments of God, so that when Our Lord shall come, thou mayest meet Him with all the Saints in the Heavenly Court, there to live forever and ever. Amen."

(The Baptismal Certificate may be kept between the pages of this book. It will be needed in years to come when other Sacraments are to be received.)

Attach photo taken on Baptismal day or Baptismal certificate in an unsealed envelope.

The Significance of the Articles Used in Baptism

The candle symbolizes Christ, whose life was consumed out of love for us.

The white cloth signifies purity of soul.

The blessed salt shows that the grace of Baptism gives a relish for heavenly knowledge.

The holy oil or Chrism is the sign of a Christian's strength.

Water signifies washing away Original Sin.

My Family

These are the full names and birthdates of my family members and something special about each one:

My Family Album

Special Photos of my Family.

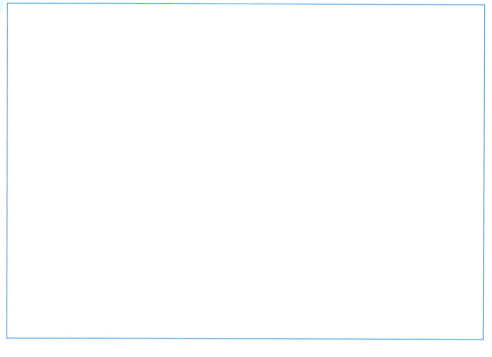

Every child is different, a special creation of God.

My very own handprint

My very own footprint

A lock of hair

One of my first visits to the Doctor took place when I was _____ .

Doctor _____ said that I _____

_____ .

Prints can be made by placing the hands or feet on a regular inking pad.

Milestones

I smiled when I was

_____ old.

I grasped an object at the age

of _____.

I cut my first tooth at

_____.

I learned to use a spoon at age _____.

I began to crawl when I was _____.

I stood alone when I was _____.

I took my first step at _____.

I climbed stairs when I was _____.

Attach photo here.

Here I am when I was _____
_____.

My first word was _____
_____.

My favorite toy was _____
_____.

My First Home

Attach picture of first home here.

I have no picture of my spiritual home in Heaven because, as Saint Paul said, no eye has seen nor has any ear heard what God has prepared for those who love Him.

My first visits to the church after Baptism were when no one else was there—only God and Mother and me. Mother showed me the light that burns for Him.
Mother lighted a ruby-red vigil lamp and knelt before the statue of Our Blessed Mother and asked her to watch over me.

I first attended Holy Mass when I was _____ .

Attach picture of church here.

My Parish Church

First Prayers

MY Mother and Father showed me beautiful pictures portraying the life of our Dear Saviour. They helped me know and love God so much that I wanted to talk to Him often.

Whenever I passed the church I would say, "Dear God, I love You."

I prayed my first prayer at age _____. I learned the "Our Father," the "Hail Mary" and the "Glory Be," and I took part in the Family Rosary when I was _____ years old.

My first celebration of the birth of Baby Jesus at Christmas took place when I was _____ old.

My Mother

Attach picture of
Mother and child here.

I think that God once took the beauty of a flower
   that does not bloom for praise, but which makes sweet some bower;
The understanding of the dew which gently falls to earth,
   reviving all the weary things and giving them new birth;
The gladness of bright dawns, a quiet evening's peace,
   the patience for the daily tasks that do not have release;
The life that finds its greatest joy in service to another;
   I think God took these priceless things and made of them—
     my Mother.
                             —Beatrice Ryan

My Father

Attach picture of
Father and child here.

My father made me see the beauty of the sky,
   the sun, the moon and stars, the heights that birds can fly.
We'd walk together in the woods, with blossoms all along
   and then we'd pause a little while to hear a bluebird's song.
He made me see the beauty, too, of smiles and words sincere.
   He made me stand both firm and strong without a doubt or fear.
He taught me that the wish to do a kindly deed
   would fill my heart with happiness and please dear God, indeed.
                              —Beatrice Ryan

Formation of Character

"Parents should be careful to make the right use of the authority given them by God, Whose vicars in a true sense they are."

Papal Encyclical, "The Christian Education of Youth"

My parents were as concerned about helping me to form character as they were about my physical needs. They didn't worry about the rate of my progress because they understood that I had my own special pattern to follow. We laughed and sang and played together. They knew that what I needed most of all was to be loved.

Qualities My Parents Wanted Me To Develop

Co-operation

My parents encouraged my attempts to be helpful.

I first helped them by _____

_____

_____

_____.

Courage

My parents told me of my ever-present Guardian Angel, which helped me to be unafraid. I first showed courage by _____

_____

_____

_____.

Generosity

I was taught that whenever I gave and whatever I shared, this was pleasing to God because it brought happiness to others. One time I _____

_____

_____

_____.

Gratitude

Even for the smallest favors I was taught to say, "Thank you," and really mean it.
I began to say, "Thank you" of my own accord when I was _____ years old.

Honesty

I was taught that to take what did not belong to me was an offense against the law of God.
I told the truth though it was very hard to do when

_____

_____

_____.

Imagination

We often played "make believe" and imagined all sorts of things. One of my first stories was about _____

_____

_____.

One of my favorite games was _____

_____.

Initiative

I was encouraged to make things in my own way.

I enjoyed making _____

_____

when I was _____ years old.

Obedience

Some of my first rules were: _____

_____

_____

_____.

Purity

I was reminded that by Baptism my body became a temple of the Holy Ghost, to be guarded and cherished as such.

Perseverance

I was expected to finish whatever I started, but I sometimes needed a little help. Some of my early projects were:

_____

_____

_____.

Other Special Memories

(These pages may be used for writing down charming sayings spoken by the little one or for recording other special moments and special events.)

Other Special Memories

Birthdays

On the eve of each birthday my Mother lighted a vigil lamp in front of the statue of Our Blessed Mother. It burned all during the Family Rosary. It burned all night long. When it flickered out, I was a year older. Birthdays were very special days, with a big candle-lighted cake and ice cream, and friends to share them.

One Year   Height _____ Weight _____
Special things to remember: _____
_____
_____

Two Years   Height _____ Weight _____
Special things to remember: _____
_____
_____

Three Years   Height _____ Weight _____
Special things to remember: _____
_____
_____

Birthdays

Four Years   Height _____   Weight _____
Special things to remember: _____
_____
_____

Five Years   Height _____   Weight _____
Special things to remember: _____
_____
_____

Six Years   Height _____   Weight _____
Special things to remember: _____
_____
_____

Seven Years   Height _____   Weight _____
Special things to remember: _____
_____
_____

Eight Years   Height _____   Weight _____
Special things to remember: _____
_____
_____

My First School

Attach picture of school
or schoolroom here.

Name of School _____ Place _____

My Teacher's name was _____

My first response to school was _____

My First Confession

For some time I had known right from wrong. I had not always chosen right, but now I received new proof of God's love for me, the Sacrament of Penance, which took away my sins and gave me new graces to strengthen my good intentions. I made my First Confession at age _____ on

_____,

to Father _____

at _____ Church.

My First Holy Communion

I received Our Lord in Holy Communion for the first time on _____ from Father _____ at _____Church, when I was _____ years old.

I was enrolled in the Brown Scapular of Our Lady of Mount Carmel by Father _____ on _____.

I received the Sacrament of Confirmation from Bishop _____ at _____ Church on _____.

# Photographs

Photographs

Prayers

Angel of God

ANGEL of God, my guardian dear,
 To whom His love commits me here,
Ever this day be at my side,
 To light and guard, to rule and guide.
 Amen.

From *The Little Key to Heaven*

Grace before Meals

BLESS US, O Lord, and these Thy gifts,
 Which we are about to receive from
Thy bounty.
Through Christ Our Lord.
Amen.